THE LEWIS AND CLARK EXPEDITION
Coloring Book

Peter F. Copeland

Dover Publications, Inc., New York

Introduction

The Louisiana Purchase of 1803 brought the young republic of the United States a vast western territory which extended from the Mississippi River all the way to the Rocky Mountains. President Thomas Jefferson determined to send an expedition to explore the huge wilderness area that had now become part of the nation. Captains Meriwether Lewis and William Clark of the U.S. Army headed an expedition of forty-five experienced woodsmen, hunters and soldiers, which sailed up the Missouri River from St. Louis in May 1804.

They took notes, gathered scientific specimens, drew maps and christened landmarks as they proceeded through the wilderness, trading with and making friends among the Indian tribes through whose lands they passed. The expedition spent the winter of 1804–05 in a stockade they built in the country of the Mandan Indians, in present-day North Dakota. In the spring of 1805 the expedition continued up the Missouri into the foothills of the Rocky Mountains.

The explorers crossed the high mountains and passed the Continental Divide, launching their boats into a tributary of the Columbia River, from which they reached the Pacific Ocean in early November 1805. The expedition returned across the continent, reaching St. Louis in September 1806, ending an eight-thousand-mile journey which lasted over two years. Loaded with information about this vast and unknown territory, they had successfully completed one of the most difficult experiences of exploration ever undertaken.

Published in Canada by General Publishing Company, Ltd., 30 Lesmill Road, Don Mills, Toronto, Ontario.

Published in the United Kingdom by Constable and Company, Ltd., 10 Orange Street, London WC2H 7EG.

The Lewis and Clark Expedition Coloring Book is a new work, first published by Dover Publications, Inc., in 1983.

International Standard Book Number: 0-486-24557-8

Manufactured in the United States of America
Dover Publications, Inc., 31 East 2nd Street, Mineola, N.Y. 11501

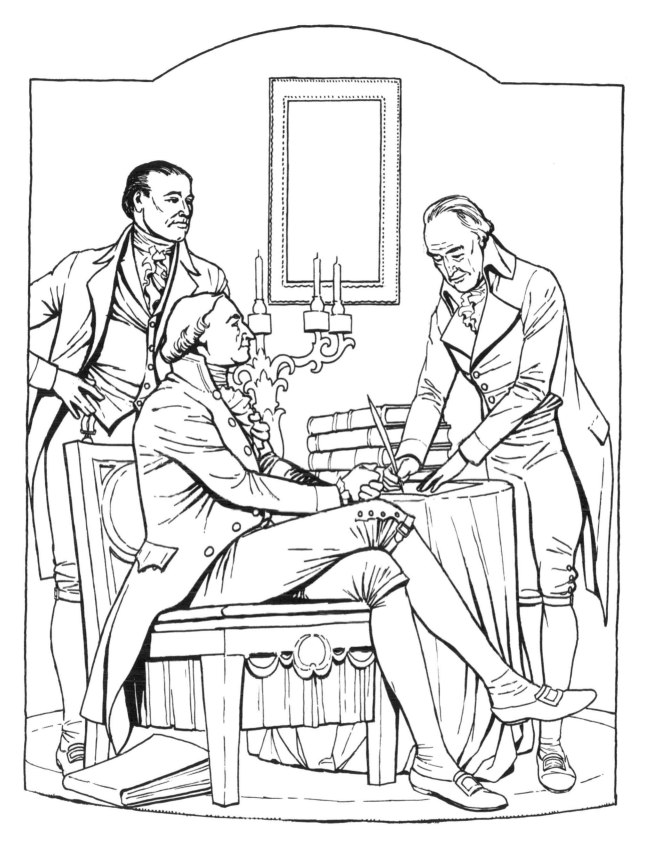

1. Signing the Louisiana Purchase Agreement in Paris, April 30, 1803. The Louisiana Territory, sold by France to the United States, contained more than 825,000 square miles of largely unexplored land stretching from New Orleans north to the Canadian border and west from the Mississippi River to the Rocky Mountains. President Thomas Jefferson paid the French Emperor Napoleon approximately eighteen cents a square mile for this vast wilderness territory. The purchase of this land doubled the size of the United States.

2. On May 14, 1804 Captains Meriwether Lewis and William Clark set sail up the Missouri River with a little fleet of three vessels. They had been commissioned by President Jefferson to form an expedition and explore the newly purchased wilderness territory. From the beginning the going was difficult. The explorers had to make their way upriver, in heavily loaded boats, against high water and a fast current.

3. The members of the Lewis and Clark expedition were all skilled men: hunters, carpenters, gunsmiths and blacksmiths, experienced and well equipped for a life in the wilderness. The explorer on the right carries an air gun, which could fire forty shots from a single charge of compressed air carried in the metal ball in front of the trigger.

4. At the French riverside village of St. Charles, expedition members enjoyed themselves at a dance given by the local residents. This would be their last view of civilization for more than two years.

5. Often the explorers had to drag the boats through strong river currents filled with sandbars and snags of fallen trees, constantly fighting off swarms of mosquitoes and other insects. Wolves and rattlesnakes were seen along the banks of the river.

6. The explorers trapped many beavers for food along the banks of the Missouri River. Beaver steaks were considered a great delicacy. The popularity of beaver hats among gentlemen in the East and in Europe soon led trappers into the area. They took the beavers for their pelts in such numbers that by 1830 very few beavers were to be seen along the river.

7. The burial of Sergeant Floyd, August 20, 1804. It is remarkable that only one death occurred among the members of the expedition during the entire voyage. Sergeant Floyd, who is believed to have died of a ruptured appendix, was buried on a bluff above the Missouri. One half mile away from his grave, in the present state of Iowa, flows a small river which bears his name.

8. In August the explorers held their first council with the Indians of the Great Plains, in the present state of Nebraska. On September 25, 1804 Captain Clark reported an angry encounter with some Indian warriors in what is now South Dakota. "The second chief was very insolent, both in words and gestures . . . . I felt myself compelled to draw my sword," Clark wrote. Normally encounters between members of the expedition and Indians were friendly and often they were festive affairs.

9. Captain Clark carried to an Indian village, September 26, 1804. When the explorers came ashore in the land of the Teton Sioux, Captain Clark was carried ceremoniously to their village by the Indians on an elegantly painted buffalo robe, an honor that the Sioux reserved for visiting chiefs.

10. Here is a leader of the Dog Band of Hidatsa warriors, a fierce tribal society, engaged in a dance, from a painting done twenty-nine years after the Lewis and Clark expedition visited them.

11. Assiniboine Indians. Among the Indian tribes with whom the explorers traded in the winter of 1804 were the Assiniboines, who lived in what is now North Dakota. The Plains Indians had acquired guns and other trade goods from both the French and English, with whom they had been in occasional contact for many years.

12. Elk along the Missouri river. The country through which the expedition passed was thick with game, "immense herds of buffalo, deer, elk, and antelopes, which we saw in every direction," wrote Meriwether Lewis in September 1804.

13. A hunting party of Sioux warriors. The Sioux Indians with whom Lewis and Clark came into contact were a fierce and warlike people who hunted and killed grizzly bears as much for pleasure as for meat.

14. Indian warfare. Lewis and Clark reported constant warfare among the Indian tribes through whose country they passed. Here two painted war parties meet outside a burning village with muskets, bows and arrows, lances and scalping knives.

15. Returning to Fort Mandan from a buffalo hunt, December 1804. In November 1804 the expedition members built a fort on the east bank of the Missouri in what is today the state of North Dakota. Hunting parties ventured into the bitter cold, bringing back buffalo and deer through the deep snow, to provide food for the long winter months.

16. The explorers passed the hard winter at Fort Mandan, struggling to find firewood and food, making clothes and building canoes in temperatures that sometimes reached forty degrees below zero. Here the men work at cutting their boats loose from the ice.

17. Indian medicine sign for buffalo. The Indians of the Plains depended for their survival upon the buffalo, which provided shelter, clothing, food and tools from its meat, hide and bones. Here a buffalo skull is mounted on stones to attract the herds back to the area.

18. Explorers join the Indians in a buffalo hunt. Members of the Lewis and Clark expedition often joined the Indians in hunting forays. The Indians generally hunted on horseback, killing the buffalo with bows and arrows and lances, while the explorers hunted with long Kentucky-style flintlock rifles.

19. The Indians meet a black man. Most of the Indians of the northern Plains had met white men before, but had never seen a black man. Captain Clark's slave, York, fascinated the Plains Indians, who examined him with great curiosity. To the Indians of the far Northwest, who had never seen white or black people, York was no more unusual than any of the other expedition members.

20. Mounted Blackfoot warrior. The Blackfoot Indians of the northern Plains were first encountered by the Lewis and Clark expedition in 1804. Buffalo hunters who had learned to domesticate the wild horses of the Plains in the 1700s, the Blackfoot wore fringed buckskin shirts decorated with porcupine quills dyed red and yellow. Many Blackfoot warriors hunted with the bow and arrow but some had acquired such items as muskets and gunpowder from the white traders.

21. Buffalo Dance of the Mandan Indians. Captain Clark reported seeing a buffalo dance that lasted for three days in one village. The dance, in which painted warriors represented buffalo and hunters, was intended to attract buffalo in times when game was scarce.

22. Sacajawea, or "Bird Woman." Her husband, Toussaint Charbonneau, and their infant son Jean-Baptiste accompanied the Lewis and Clark expedition from the Mandan country of present-day North Dakota to the coast of Oregon. Sacajawea served the expedition as a guide, and she and her husband were interpreters among the Indians they encountered on their way to the Pacific coast.

23. On April 10, 1805, Lewis and Clark met with three French trappers who were hunting beaver. The trappers asked to accompany the expedition as far as the Yellowstone River so as to be safe from a possible Indian attack.

24. Sergeant Ordway, one of the explorers, reported on May 14, 1805 that one of the expedition hunters was chased and nearly caught by a large wounded bear. Captain Lewis wrote, "I had rather fight two Indians than one bear."

25. Encounters with dangerous animals were not uncommon. Captain Lewis reported that a large bull buffalo stampeded along the river bank one night in May 1805, running through the expedition's camp and narrowly missing several of the men. His course was only deflected by the barking of the Captain's dog.

26. On May 26, 1805 Meriwether Lewis got his first view of the Rocky Mountains. "I felt a secret pleasure in finding myself so near the head of the heretofore conceived boundless Missouri," he wrote in his journal.

27. In early June Captain Lewis saved the life of one of his men, Richard Windsor, who slipped on a rain-soaked cliff edge above the North Fork of the Missouri, and saved himself only by obeying the Captain's careful instructions, slowly inching his way back to safety and digging toeholds in the cliff face with his knife.

28. A herd of bighorn sheep grazing in the hills before the strange sandstone cliffs carved by the wind and rain of centuries. They were seen by Lewis and Clark from the banks of the Missouri in the spring of 1805.

29. On June 21, 1805 the explorers set out overland to pass the Great Falls of the Missouri. Under a burning sun the men hauled boats and supplies around the falls in two weeks of heavy labor before they reached the river again and could launch their boats.

30. Members of a Piegan Indian war party on a horse-stealing expedition ride toward the foothills of what is today northern Montana. Horse stealing among the Piegans was an honorable act of warfare. (Here the Lewis and Clark Expedition passed the Continental Divide, which marked the western edge of the Louisiana Territory.)

31. Interior of a Mandan Indian hut. The houses of the Mandans were round and very wide, made of a sort of "picket work," as Captain Clark reported in October 1804. Such a house would contain several families, all their belongings and their animals.

32. In late September 1805 the explorers camped opposite the forks of the Missouri and set to work building five canoes. Since many of the men were weak with sickness, they adopted the labor-saving Indian method of hollowing out logs by fire, shaping them into dugout canoes.

33. Captain Clark is seen here taking a position sight with the brass-bound compass he carried in a leather case throughout the expedition. This compass is now in the collection of the Smithsonian Institution in Washington, D.C.

34. Captain William Clark meets the Shoshoni Chief Cameahwait, and the guide Sacajawea is reunited with her family and tribe after many years of separation. The chief placed a skin mantle around Clark's neck and Captain Clark put his cocked hat and feather on the head of the chief.

35. In the snowy fastnesses of the Bitterroot Mountain Range the explorers suffered severely from the cold, and feared that their feet, clad only in thin moccasins, would freeze. Game in these mountains was so scarce that the explorers were forced to eat several of their horses.

36. Running the Short Narrows of the Columbia River. A high black rock narrowed the current of the Columbia to forty-five yards, producing swift rapids. Daunted by the prospect of hauling their boats and equipment over the high rock, the explorers decided to run the narrows, which they did successfully, to the astonishment of the Indians who had gathered to watch them.

37. A village of the Colville Indians near Kettle Falls on the Columbia River was visited by the explorers in October 1805. These Indians subsisted mainly on the abundant schools of salmon in the Columbia, which they dried for use during the winter months.

38. On November 3, 1805 the explorers sighted majestic Mount Hood. Captain Clark noted that the mountain stood about "forty-seven miles from the mouth of the Quicksilver River."

39. The explorers met Chinook Indians near the mouth of the Columbia River. Captain Clark wrote, "I observed two beautiful canoes, tapered to each end, on the bow curious figures were cut in the wood."

40. On November 7, 1805 the explorers had their first view of the Pacific Ocean. Captain Clark wrote, "We are in view of the Ocean, this great Pacific Ocean which we have been so long anxious to see and the roaring or noise made by the waves breaking upon the rocky shore may be heard distinctly." After wintering on the Oregon coast, the explorers began the long journey back to St. Louis on March 23, 1806.

41. On July 27, 1806 there was a fight between expedition members and a party of Piegan warriors in which two of the Indians were left dead, the only Indians killed by the explorers during the entire course of the expedition.

42. In August of 1806 the expedition was again in the country of the Mandan Indians. Captain Clark made a present to the Indians of the swivel gun that had been mounted in the bows of one of the keelboats and was no longer needed by the homeward-bound explorers.

43. Captain Meriwether Lewis was shot in the leg accidentally by a fellow hunter while searching for game in a forest in what is now North Dakota. "I instantly supposed that Cruzette (the other hunter) had shot me in mistake for an elk, as I was dressed in brown leather," wrote Lewis on August 11, 1806. The wound proved not to be serious.

44. At last, on September 20, 1806, the boats of the Lewis and Clark expedition reached the little village of La Charette, near St. Charles, on the Missouri. They were almost home. The men fired off their guns joyfully as they headed into shore. At La Charette the explorers learned that they had long since been given up as lost forever in the wilderness.

45. William Clark (*top*) and Meriwether Lewis. Meriwether Lewis, once private secretary to Thomas Jefferson, and his friend, William Clark, brother of Revolutionary war hero George Rogers Clark, were both experienced explorers and well versed in the natural sciences of their day. The famous expedition they headed brought back a large collection of scientific information, opened the unknown West to American exploration and settlement and added credibility to the United States claim to the Oregon Territory. Other men would follow the trail they blazed through the West, but they were the first, and their story is like no other in our history.

DOVER COLORING BOOKS

AUDUBON'S BIRDS OF AMERICA COLORING BOOK, John James Audubon. (23049-X) $2.00

THE CAT COLORING BOOK, Karen Baldauski. (24011-8) $2.25

THE WONDERFUL WIZARD OF OZ COLORING BOOK, L. Frank Baum. (20452-9) $2.00

BIBLE STORIES COLORING BOOK. (20623-8) $2.00

GARDEN FLOWERS COLORING BOOK, Stefen Bernath. (23142-9) $2.00 TROPICAL FISH COLORING BOOK, Stefen Bernath. (23620-X) $2.00

TREES OF THE NORTHEAST COLORING BOOK, Stefen Bernath. (23734-6) $2.25

FIFTY FAVORITE BIRDS COLORING BOOK, Lisa Bonforte. (24261-7) $2.25

ALICE IN WONDERLAND COLORING BOOK, Lewis Carroll. (22853-3) $2.00

ANTIQUE AIRPLANES COLORING BOOK, Peter F. Copeland. (21524-5) $2.00

PIRATES AND BUCCANEERS COLORING BOOK, Peter F. Copeland. (23393-6) $2.00

UNIFORMS OF THE NAPOLEONIC WARS COLORING BOOK, Peter F. Copeland. (24390-7) $2.50

SEASHORE LIFE COLORING BOOK, Anthony D'Attilio. (22930-0) $1.95

AIRPLANES OF WORLD WAR I COLORING BOOK, Carlo Demand. (23807-5) $2.25

CLASSIC RACING CARS OF THE WORLD COLORING BOOK, Carlo Demand. (24294-3) $2.25

DOLLY DINGLE COLORING BOOK, Grace Drayton and Frank Fontana. (24416-4) $2.00

THE VICTORIAN SEASIDE HOTEL COLORING BOOK, Charles Fleischman & Kristin Helberg. (24399-0) $2.50

THE WIND IN THE WILLOWS COLORING BOOK: TOAD'S ADVENTURES, Kenneth Grahame. (23292-1) $2.00

MOTHER GOOSE COLORING BOOK, Kate Greenaway. (22883-5) $2.00

ABC COLORING BOOK, Richard Hefter. (22969-6) $2.00

VISUAL ILLUSIONS COLORING BOOK, Spyros Horemis. (21595-4) $2.00

ANTIQUE AUTOMOBILES COLORING BOOK, Clarence P. Hornung. (22742-1) $2.00

MYTHICAL BEASTS COLORING BOOK, Fridolf Johnson. (23353-7) $2.00

FOLK COSTUMES OF EUROPE COLORING BOOK, Susan Johnston. (23513-0) $1.95

PATCHWORK QUILT COLORING BOOK, Susan Johnston. (23845-8) $1.75

NORTH AMERICAN INDIAN DESIGN COLORING BOOK, Paul E. Kennedy. (21125-8) $1.95

Paperbound unless otherwise indicated. Prices subject to change without notice. Available at your book dealer or write for free catalogues to Dept. Coloring Books, Dover Publications, Inc., 31 East 2nd Street, Mineola, N.Y. 11501. Please indicate field of interest. Each year Dover publishes over 200 books on fine art, music, crafts and needlework, antiques, languages, literature, children's books, chess, cookery, nature, anthropology, science, mathematics, and other areas.

Manufactured in the U.S.A.